Anyone Can Teach Vowels

By LaTondra Moultrie

(c)2021, LaTondra Moultrie
All rights reserved

Anyone Can Teach is a Trademark of LaTondra Moultrie.
Trademarks may be registered in some jurisdictions.
All other trademarks are the property of their respective owners.

No claim to copyright is made for original U.S. Government Works.

No part of this document may be reproduced in any form or by any means, electronic, graphic, or mechanical, including but not limited to photocopying, information storage, and retrieval systems, without permission in writing from the publisher.

- **Study with this book when your child is relaxed.**
- **If your child loses interest, stop while having fun and try again later.**
- **Praise your child's success.**

- There are twenty-six letters in the alphabet. five of those letters are vowels, twenty-one are constants.

- Practice the alphabet each day, until your child recognizes each letter of the alphabet.

- Introduce vowels, (a,e,i,o,u).

- Introduce consonants, (B,C,D,F,G,H,J,K,L,M,N,P,Q,R,S,T,V,W,X,Y,Z).

- Learn vowel sounds, vowels have two sounds, a short sound, and a long sound.

Aa Bb Cc Dd Ee
Ff Gg Hh Ii Jj Kk
Ll Mm Nn Oo Pp
Qq Rr Ss Tt Uu
Vv Ww Xx Yy Zz

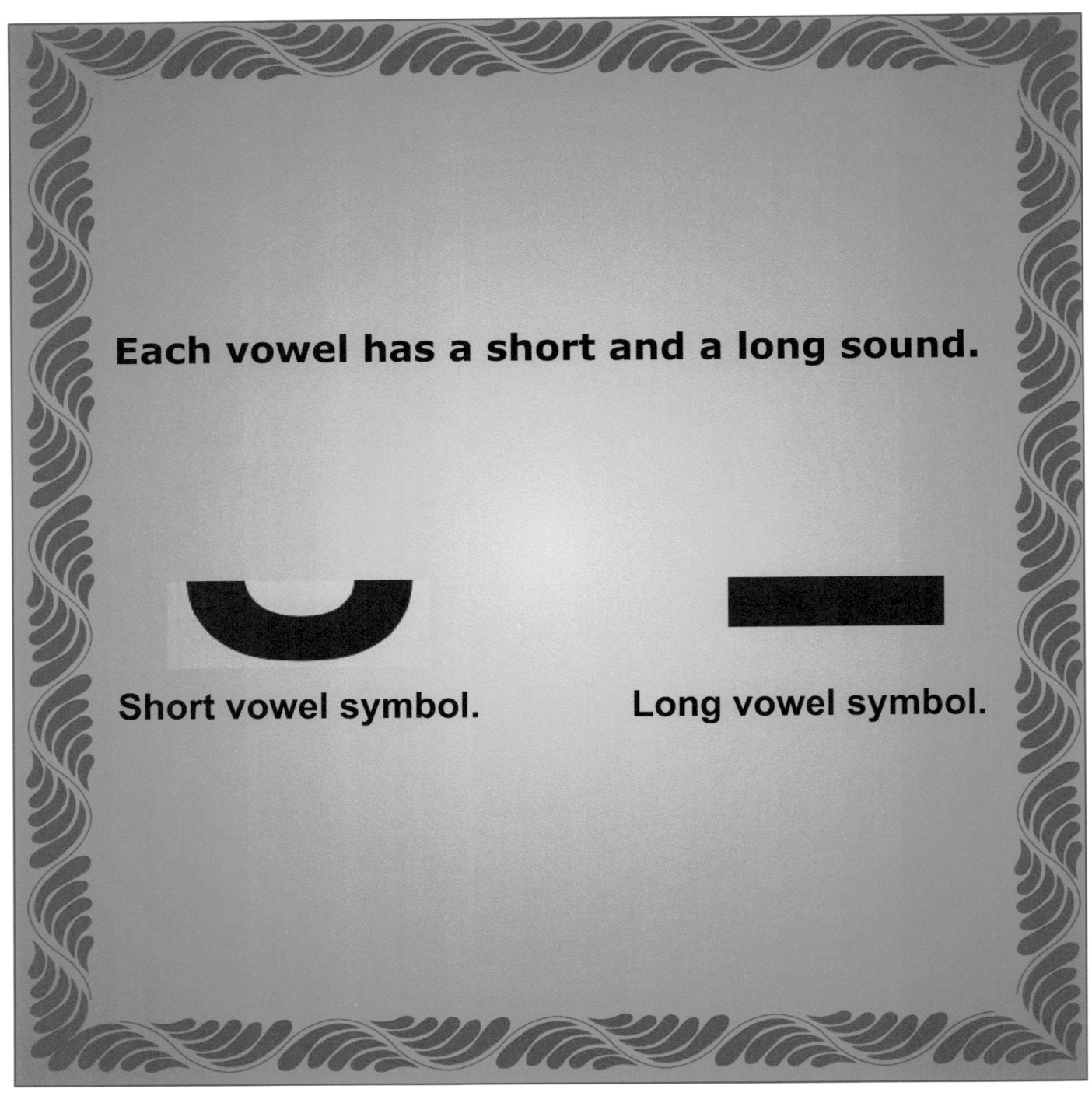

Long Vowels

Long vowel sounds are easy to pronounce, they sound like the letter.

The word <u>apricot</u> makes the long a sound.

The word <u>eagle</u> makes the long e sound.

Ī
i

The word <u>ice cream</u> makes the long I sound.

ō

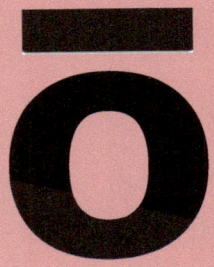

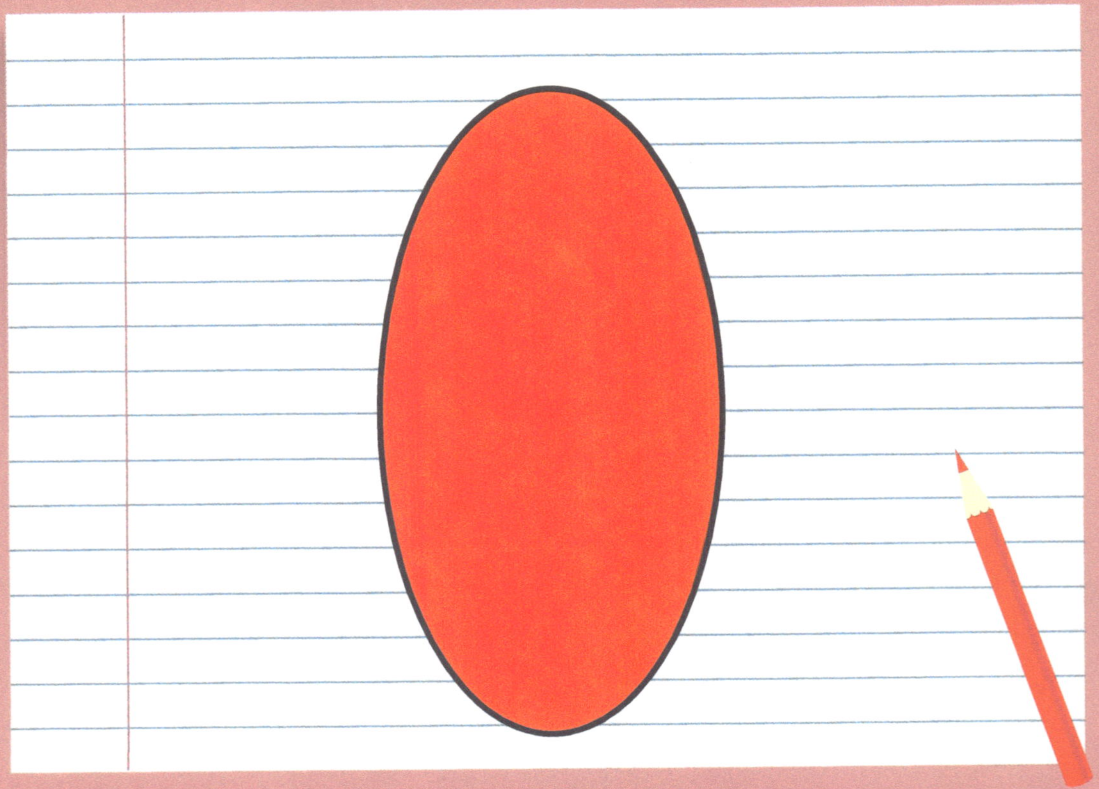

The word <u>oval</u> makes the long o sound.

The word <u>uniform</u> makes the long u sound.

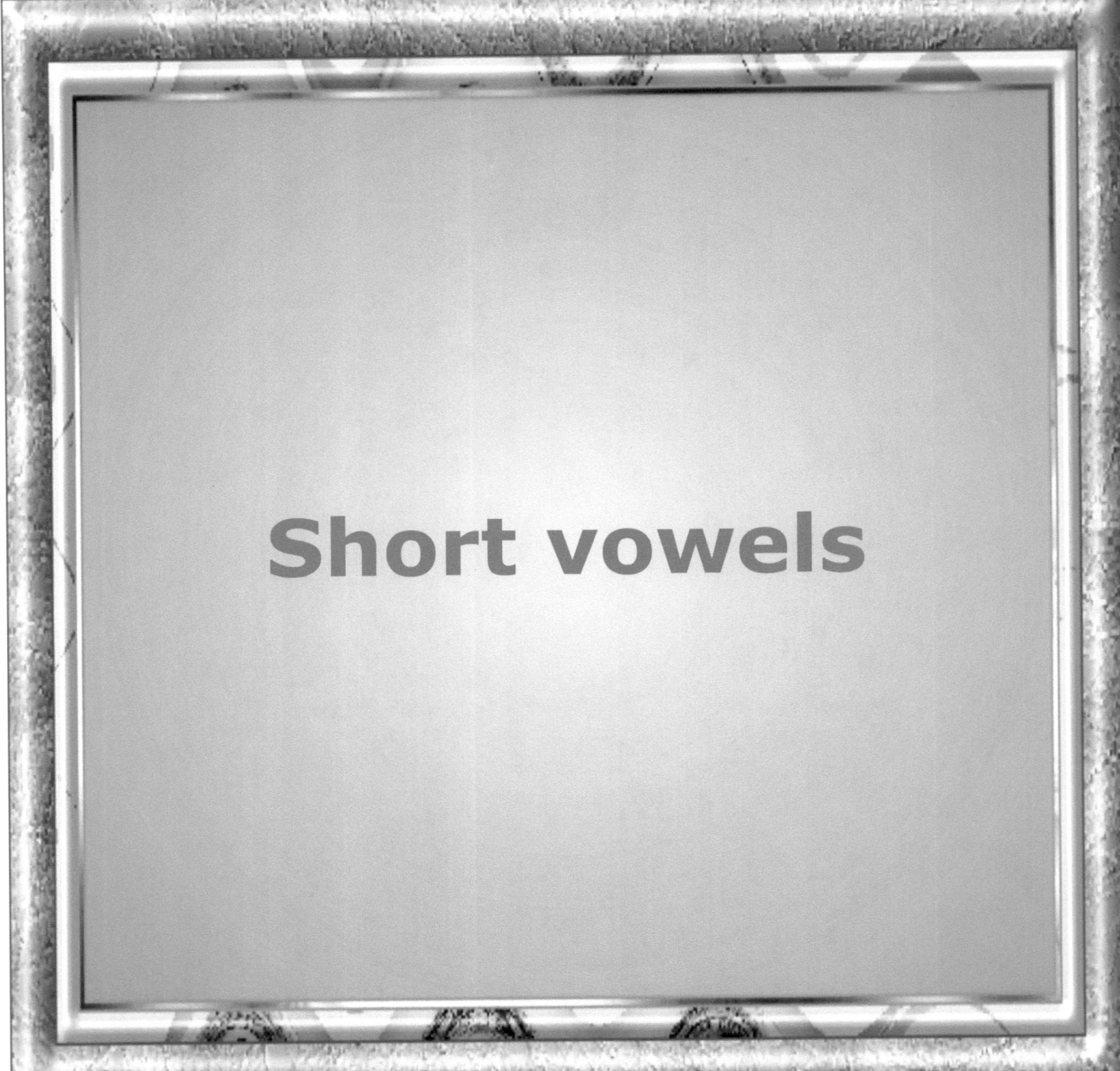

ă

The word <u>alligator</u> makes the short a sound. To make the short a sound, open your mouth wide, keep your tongue on the floor of your mouth and push air out.

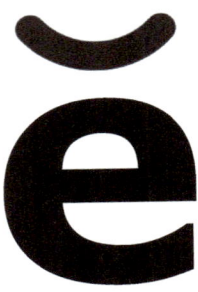

The word <u>elephant</u> makes the short e sound. To make the short e sound, slightly spread your lips and let the air out.

The word <u>ink</u> makes the short I sound. To make the short I sound very slightly open your mouth and quickly push out a puff of air.

The word <u>ostrich</u> makes the short o sound. To make the short o sound open your mouth and round your lips, let the air flow out of your mouth.

The word <u>umbrella</u> makes the short u sound. To make the short u sound, slightly open your mouth and gently let the air flow out.

www.ingramcontent.com/pod-product-compliance
Lightning Source LLC
Chambersburg PA
CBHW040024050426
42452CB00002B/116